The EPIC Series

Text © Michael Brennan
Images © Catarina Neto

www.theepicseries.com

@theepicseriesofficial

To my ski and snowboard family. You know who you are!

The EPIC Powder Day

written by
Michael Brennan

illustrated by
Catarina Neto

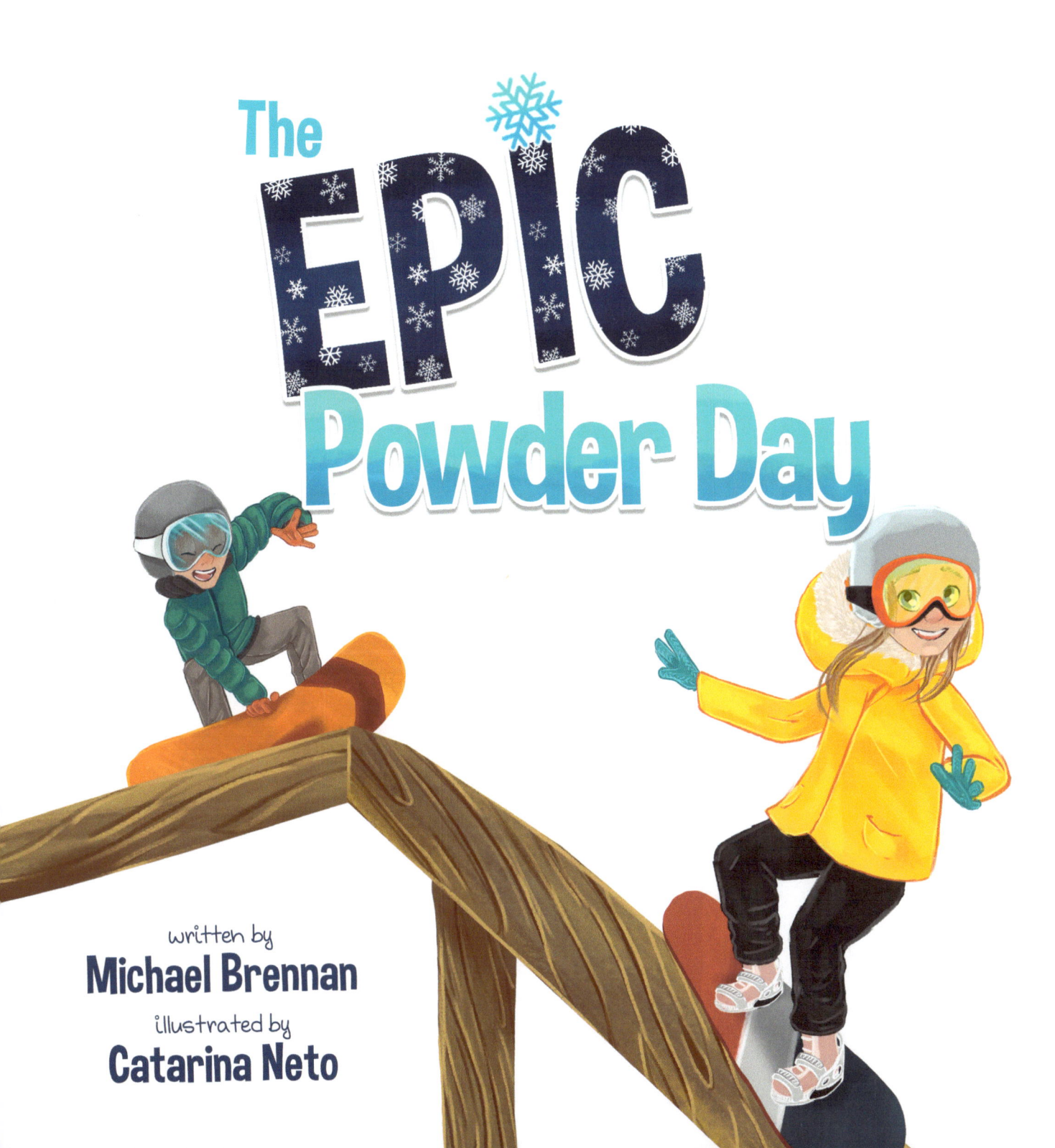

It snowed overnight!
Car's already packed.
There's no time for breakfast,
So, grab a quick snack.

The lot has been plowed.
Flakes continue to fall.
We wanted first tracks,
But ski patrol beat us all!

Let's hop on the lift,
Now look down below.
Ten inches of powder,
There's so much snow!

Strap into your snowboards.
We'll click into our skis.
Can you believe it?
It's up to our knees!

EXPERT ◆ ◄

INTERMEDIATE ■ ↑

BEGINNER ● ➡

Should we try a green circle,
Black diamond, blue square?
There's a trail map.
Let's traverse over there!

With so many runs
And plenty of options,
What's the quickest way down?
You know we're not stoppin'!

This one is perfect.
It's a straight shot.
We'll race you down.
Ready or not!

So, the skiers took off
With style and steeze.
They found a short cut
And went through the trees.

TERRAIN PARK

FREESTYLE
TERRAIN
THIS PARK CONTRAINS
S M L
FEATURES

The snowboarders followed
With eyes on their mark.
A short cut of their own,
Freshly groomed terrain park.

The glades were quite tight,
Very narrow, and steep.
But the skiers were good.
Could shred it in their sleep.

The park was tricked out
With long rails and huge jumps.
The boarders hit grinds
Then traded fist bumps.

The skiers were ahead.
Thought they'd won without fail.
But the boarders never gave up
And were right on their tail.

Then the trails merged.
The black diamond was double.
With moguls ahead,
Everyone was in trouble!

So, down they went,
But soon had to bail.
They all caught an edge
And yelled out "yard sale!"

There they were stuck
In the fluffy deep powder.
"We can't see our stuff!"
They could not have laughed louder!

Let's call it a tie.
An offer no one could dodge.
So, they cleaned up their gear
And headed into the lodge.

The hot cocoa was warm
And the fire was blazing.
Everyone agreed,
This powder day was amazing.

How would you rank it?
A true ten out of ten.
There's more snow in the forecast,
So, let's do it again!

Overview & About The Author

The Epic Powder Day is the second book in "The Epic Series" by Michael Brennan and is a children's book that was inspired by Mike's annual winter family vacations to the Pocono Mountains. He seeks to highlight the excitement of a snow day, push back against the distractions of screens and technology, and be fully present in the moment. He hopes this book will encourage children to experience the beauty in nature, encourage friendly competition, inspire adventure, and motivate kids to create their own life long memories. Mike currently resides in Bucks County, Pennsylvania, with his beautiful wife, Kimberly, and their son, Brayden. His hobbies include traveling, soccer, pickleball, skiing, and enjoying family walks.

Acknowledgments

Thanks to my wife, Kim, for believing that I could turn this idea into a finished product as well as continuing to support me through this entire process. You are the best!

Thanks to my dad who did everything possible to ensure I had the best childhood and was surrounded by the family and support system that I needed growing up. I love you!

Thanks to the entire Brennan family for the times that we spent up the Poconos. Every year, I would look forward to missing school for a couple days to explore a new mountain house. So many funny stories and unforgettable memories were made along the way; including the diaper rugs, snow dances, and hanging out in the hot tub just to name a few. I love you all!

Thanks to the entire Pohl family for letting me experience the mountain house at such a young age. During high school and into college, New Year's became one of my favorite holidays because I got to spend it with you all out on the mountain. I love you guys!

Thanks again to my illustrator, Catarina. You brought my vision to life and I am forever thankful that I found you. You are a great communicator, pay close attention to detail, and take great pride in your final product. I look forward to working with you on another Epic Series release!